D0537878

WALKS IN THE SURREY HILLS

WALKS IN THE SURREY HILLS

*Janet Spayne and
Audrey Krynski*

COUNTRYSIDE BOOKS
NEWBURY, BERKSHIRE

First published 1974
by Spurbooks

Second edition published 1991
Fully revised and updated 1996, 2004
© Janet Spayne and Audrey Krynski 2004

COUNTRYSIDE BOOKS
3 Catherine Road
Newbury, Berkshire

Publisher's Note

We hope that you obtain considerable enjoyment from this book; great care has been taken in its preparation. Although at the time of publication all routes followed public rights of way or permitted paths, diversion orders can be made and permissions withdrawn.

We cannot, of course, be held responsible for such diversion orders and any inaccuracies in the text which result from these or any other changes to the routes nor any damage which might result from walkers trespassing on private property. We are anxious though that all details covering the walks are kept up to date and would therefore welcome information from readers which would be relevant to future editions.

The simple sketch maps that accompany the walks in this book are based on notes made by the author whilst checking out the routes on the ground. They are designed to show you how to reach the start and to point out the main features of the overall circuit.

However, for the benefit of a proper map, we do recommend that you purchase the relevant Ordnance Survey sheet covering your walk. The Ordnance Survey maps are widely available, especially through booksellers and local newsagents.

ISBN 1 85306 120 4

Cover photograph of Brockham Village
by Andy Williams

Produced through MRM Associates Ltd., Reading
Printed in England by J. W. Arrowsmith Ltd., Bristol

Contents

AREA MAP

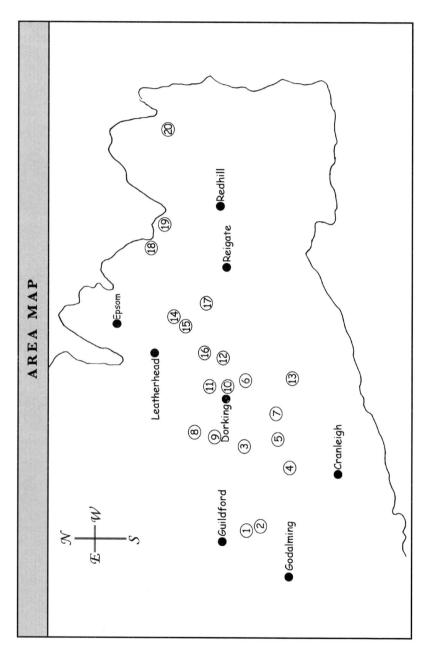

COUNTRY CODE

1. Guard against all risks of fire.
2. Fasten all gates.
3. Keep dogs under proper control.
4. Keep to the paths across farmland.
5. Avoid damaging fences.
6. Leave no litter.
7. Safeguard water supplies.
8. Protect wild life, wild plants and trees.
9. Go carefully on country roads.
10. Respect the life of the countryside.

INTRODUCTION

It is almost 30 years since we first compiled this book of walks taking our readers to popular places by less frequented paths. Inevitably, many changes have taken place – not least the growth of trees which now hide what were once wide views. Heathland with low scrub is now covered in tall trees and, whilst providing shade, does restrict what we can see.

We have rewalked and updated all the walks, making considerable changes to some of them, which will make the walks more enjoyable. With the growth in popularity of walking, some paths, over the years, have become wider and much easier to follow.

The walks in this book explore only a small part of Surrey but provide examples of its wide variety of countryside – farmland, heathland, woods, water, downland and a large number of areas of outstanding natural beauty. Explorer maps 145 and 146 cover all the walks and, though not essential, will greatly add to the enjoyment in following the routes.

The chalky downland of Surrey is home to a variety of wild flowers including many species of orchids, whilst the more acid greensand gives us swathes of heather in August.

All the walks in this book are real country walks along the lesser used paths. Stout and water-resistant footwear is always recommended therefore, especially during the winter months or after wet weather. Happy walking!

Janet Spayne
Spring 2004

10

THE SILENT POOL

St Martha's, Chilworth
6 miles (or two walks of 3 miles)

This ramble in the Tillingbourne Valley takes us through woodland, downland and farmland. We see the remains of the gunpowder industry for which Chilworth was once famous and pass the millponds with their wildlife. Very little mud will be encountered.

This is a figure of eight walk, which can be started from either the Silent Pool or Chilworth railway station – the two loops making shorter 3-mile walks.

How to get there: By bus to the junction of the A25 and the A248. By train to Chilworth where the walk can be joined. By car to the car park at the Silent Pool.

Starting from Chilworth Station:
We leave the station and turn left along the main road for approximately 100 yards where we take a footpath on the right next to a school. We cross a bridge over the river, taking the right fork to a crossing track where we turn right, keeping straight ahead to a high bank of earth. Now continue the walk from (**X**).

WALK 1

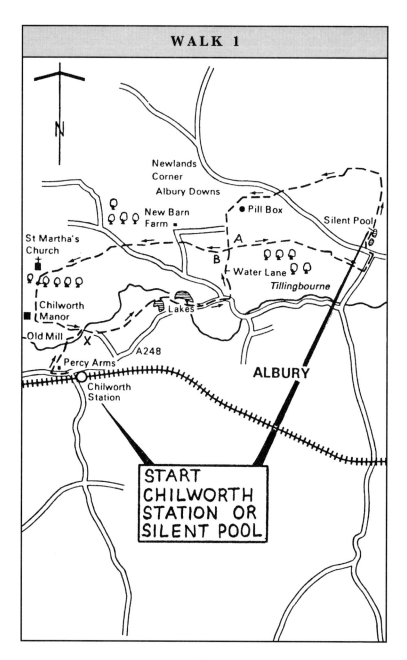

Starting from the Silent Pool:

After visiting the Silent Pool, which is very deep and fed by underground springs, we return to the entrance and turn right on the track with the pool on our right, going uphill for nearly half a mile to a wide crossing track at the top of the hill where we turn left. Later when this forks we take the left, slightly downhill track, and keep right at the next fork. We come out to a road which we cross to go through a gate opposite bearing right over a field towards a hedge ahead. At a junction of paths, with a pillbox on the left, we turn left down a stony track bearing left just past an old quarry, and continue down the lane, passing a turning on the right which goes to New Barn Farm.

To return to the Silent Pool (short version) we take the next turning on the left and continue the walk from (**A**).

To continue the walk or for Chilworth we take a signposted bridleway on the right just past this turning.

(**B**) We later go through a gate, then take the footpath going diagonally across the field to a lane, which we cross to a fenced track, part of the old Pilgrim's Way. At a road we cross to a path slightly to the left and go left with it, turning right through a barrier and forking right uphill ignoring branching paths until St Martha's church is reached, passing on our way the Downs Link information board. The original church dated from the 12th century but fell into disrepair and was rebuilt on its original foundations in the mid 19th century.

Leaving the church by the south wicket gate between conifers, opposite the entrance to the church, we take a very steep downhill path ignoring crossing paths. Over the years this steep path has become very eroded with wear and weather and an easier way down the hill is to retrace our steps to the Downs Link information board, turn right and follow this track to the foot of the hill, where we turn left. We continue along the bridleway which eventually becomes a lane and just after passing a farm entrance on the left we turn right into woods taking the left fork and shortly keeping left by a high bank of earth.

(**X**) We continue on this path with the Tillingbourne on our right, while on our left we pass the ruins of a gunpowder mill. From the mid 17th century until the end of the First World War Chilworth was an important centre for the gunpowder industry. These woods are full of old mill stones and remains of other mills, and in the First World War a regiment of soldiers kept guard day and night on the various buildings.

The paths in these woods are not public rights of way but permissive paths granted by the Borough of Guildford.

Passing the mill buildings on our left we return to the lane where we go right over the bridge and immediately left over a stile. We cross a meadow diagonally to another stile, keeping parallel with a ditch on our right, then continue over another stile and plank bridge into a field, and straight ahead with a wire fence on the right. Another stile takes us into a private garden, which has the public footpath running close to the fence on the right. We come out into a lane where we turn left round the edge of the lake – we have seen kingfishers here. We are now on a tarmac drive and when it bends left we take a waymarked path on the right into trees, keeping the lake on our left. Shortly coming out to the road, we turn left and take the second turning on the left into Water Lane. After about half a mile we reach a signposted bridleway on the left and if we wish to return to Chilworth (short version) we take the bridleway and follow the walk from (**B**) to (**X**). (To get back to Chilworth station from the high bank of earth we turn right and where the woods open out we take the first turning on the left to a bridge over the river, continuing on a footpath up to the road by a school. Here we turn left for the Percy Arms and Chilworth station.)

To continue the walk, just beyond this bridleway on the left, we take a turning on the right for the Silent Pool.

(**A**) After passing a few houses our track goes gradually uphill, later passing an isolated cottage on the right. We continue forward over a stile and soon take a signposted footpath on the right. At the end of this path we cross a quarry road to a small enclosed path opposite. A stile takes us into an open area where we go forward to another stile and continue to the road.

The rather imposing church over on our right was built in 1840 by Henry Drummond, then owner of the nearby Albury Park Estate. He was an influential member of the Drummond banking family and was a leading figure in a curious religious group known as the Catholic Apostolic Church, causing this building to be referred to locally as the 'Apostles Chapel'.

We cross the road and turn left beside a hedge to the nearby A25 with the car park diagonally left.

Refreshments: The Percy Arms inn, opposite the station in Chilworth.

WALK 2

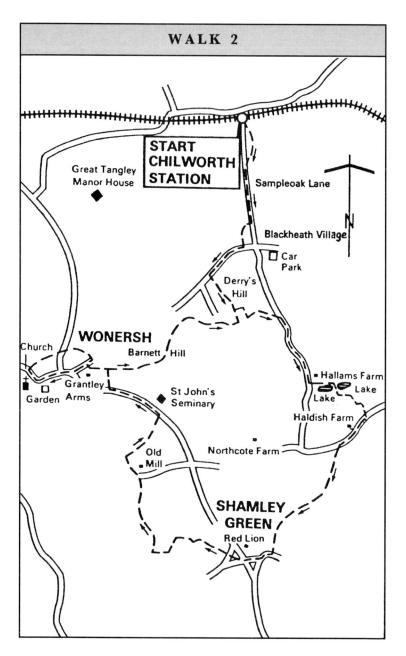

START CHILWORTH STATION

Great Tangley Manor House

Sampleoak Lane

Blackheath Village

Car Park

Derry's Hill

WONERSH

Church

Barnett Hill

Grantley Arms

Garden

St John's Seminary

Hallams Farm

Lake

Lake

Haldish Farm

Northcote Farm

Old Mill

SHAMLEY GREEN

Red Lion

16

CHILWORTH

Chilworth, Shamley Green, Wonersh
7³/₄ miles

This is a ramble in woodland and over heather and gorse-covered heathland, visiting two of Surrey's pretty villages, Shamley Green and Wonersh, with their 16th and 17th century houses. The walk is recommended for any time of the year and while there are bluebells in spring and heather in high summer, it is perhaps at its best on a crisp winter day with hoar frost on the ground.

How to get there: By train or bus to Chilworth railway station. By car on the A248 (off the A25) to Chilworth station, turning left up Sampleoak Lane to a crossroads, turning left again to a large car park.

From the car park, we return to the crossroads and keep ahead to the end of some houses and at the Blackheath sign on the right we turn left.

From the station we turn up Sampleoak Lane for about half a mile. There is a parallel footpath on the left, which avoids the first part of the road. We pass a Franciscan friary on the right and continue to the Blackheath sign. We turn right into a wide bridleway, fork left and soon turn left on a path across a heather-covered common. We continue straight ahead, ignoring a right fork, until the path bears left, passes some houses and leads us out to a road. Here we turn right and at the end of the houses on the left and at the Blackheath sign we turn left.

In about 25 yards, as this lane bears left to go behind some houses, we take a small path on the right with fields on the right behind the hedge. Soon we take the first very small path on the left, initially lined with holly bushes uphill to the top. The path bears right taking us along the ridge of the hill, giving views of St Martha's church on the hill on the left.

At a wide T-junction we turn right and, keep ahead, forking right when there is a choice to a crossing track and a wire fence round a plantation. We continue ahead taking the right fork, keeping close to the fence on our right. Immediately before a gate ahead, we turn left into a sunken path which we follow with a fence on our right until we reach a minor road. We turn right along the road and, just past some buildings, we take the signposted drive to Darbyns Brook, passing Hallams Farm on the left. Continuing along the tarmac drive, we pass a lake and a beautiful house, bearing right along a hedged track. This brings us out to a tarmac lane where we turn right, passing the attractive Haldish Farm on our right.

At Blackmoor Lodge we take a footpath on the left going gradually uphill to a crossing bridleway on Reelhall Hill. Here we turn right and immediately left thus continuing direction downhill. After two stiles in quick succession, we cross a field diagonally to two more stiles in the corner, then go down a narrow hedged path to the road.

Here we turn right for Shamley Green; a village built round two triangular village greens, most of the houses being 16th and 17th century. On reaching the first green, we turn right with the little pond on our left, then turn right along the next green with the Red Lion pub on our right. Approaching the Red Lion, we bear left across the green and go down Sweetwater Lane. In a few yards we turn right along an enclosed footpath, soon bearing right to a road where we turn left, then right, into Nursery Hill. At No.42 there is an enclosed footpath on the left which soon leaves the houses and, after going through a small plantation, enters a field. We ignore the stiles on the right and cross the field to the far corner and another stile leading to an enclosed footpath which crosses a drive and continues forward.

When we reach Cherry Tree Cottage on the left, we turn right down a track and out to the road, where again we turn right. We continue along this pleasant little road for less than half a mile and, as the road turns sharply right just after Norley House, we go over a stile to a signposted footpath on the left. We keep straight ahead, crossing a mill stream and turning right with the drive past the 15th century Mill House.

We come out to the main road and turn left past St John's Seminary and, in just under a quarter of a mile, we turn right up the steps into a field. We follow a fenced path straight across the field to go through a kissing gate, turning left down to a timbered farmhouse. We then turn left down a minor road to the main road, turning right for the centre of Wonersh, passing the 15th century Grantley Arms inn on our left, and taking the left fork, past several lovely black and white timbered houses. Through a brick archway on the left is a secluded garden given by Mrs F H Cook for the quiet use of residents. Note the interesting friezes either side of the archway.

Just past the entrance to the church on our left, we take a footpath on the right through a kissing gate by the side of a beautiful ancient timbered house. At the end of a brick wall we turn right through 'squeeze' posts down a track to a road, passing the Memorial Hall on our left. We cross the road diagonally left and, with the church hall on our right, follow the trees and a ditch on the right to another road where we turn right. In a few yards, we take the signposted footpath on our left by the timbered farmhouse we passed earlier and continue along this fenced path gradually going uphill to the top of Barnett Hill. Soon after passing the house at the top of the hill, we take an enclosed footpath on our right leading into a fenced bridleway. We continue forward passing a small chapel and graveyard on our right and later some farm buildings on our left. At a junction of paths, we turn left and continue along this path, returning to the lane we were in earlier, and out to the road. We then turn right and just past the village hall (for the car park keep straight on) take the signposted bridleway on our left, soon turning right on a track behind a house. Another track feeds in on the left and we are shortly at a crossing track where we turn right. After about

50 yards, a very narrow path turns off on our left, leading us to a track where we turn right then left into Sampleoak Lane for the station.

Refreshments: These are available at Shamley Green, with a choice of inns. At Wonersh, there is an inn and a little corner shop which sells ice-cream. There is an inn at Blackheath on the way back to the car park, and the Percy Arms, opposite Chilworth station.

GOMSHALL

Shere Heath, Albury Park 4³/₄ miles
Shere Heath, Albury Heath, Blackheath, Brook 7 miles

This is a heath, park and farmland walk, taking us past many beautiful old houses. It is suitable for any time of the year and very little mud will be encountered in this mainly sandy area.

How to get there: By train or bus to Gomshall railway station where there is a car park.

For both walks:
Leaving Gomshall station down the approach road, we cross the road with care and turn left through the pedestrian tunnel and immediately right along Wonham Way, a stony track. We cross a stream, pass a cottage on the left and, as the track turns sharply left, we turn right along a fenced path, with a large house on the right and farm buildings on the left. At the end of the path, we turn right under a railway bridge and then left along a small road to a junction. We go straight across to a signposted bridleway, Gravelpits Lane, bearing left. Opposite a house called Old Barn on the left, we turn right with another house called Highlands on the right, keeping on the right-hand path between fences, later with views of Netley House up on the right. Soon, coming into open fields with a hedge on the right, we keep straight ahead noticing Shere church down on our right. Our path comes out to a small residential road along which we continue to Shere Lane, which we cross to a

21

WALK 3

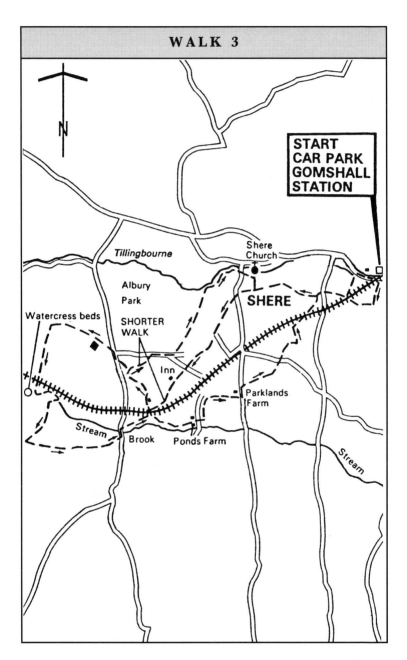

bridleway opposite which starts as a tarmac lane. This leads us through a small housing estate and into a fenced path which goes uphill into woods.

When the track forks, we take the right-hand fork, soon ignoring a left fork. After 100 yards or so, we take a clear path on the left doubling back somewhat. At a crossing track we turn right and are shortly at a small road which we cross to a footpath opposite onto Shere Heath. On reaching a junction of several paths, we go straight ahead and later down to a T-junction where we turn right, away from the railway level crossing. At a junction of paths, within sight of the road ahead, we turn left, ignoring a doubling back path on the left. This path later brings us out to the road at the William IV Inn at Little London. We turn left down the road, taking a footpath on the right just before the railway bridge.

We go up this fenced path onto Albury Heath, keeping straight ahead and passing a small red-brick building on the right. We continue along the sandy track to a wider crossing track, which we cross, and take the right fork. At a junction of paths we take the second on the right, rising gently to a crossing track with a seat.

For the shorter walk via Albury Park:

We turn right with heather heathland on our right and a few houses beyond and follow this path to a T-junction where we turn left on a rough lane to a road and turn right. We pass some houses and, as the road bears right, we take a footpath on the left through a gate into Albury Park and go down an avenue of fine chestnut trees. After a stile and a gate beside the lodge, we keep along the track with the ford and river on our left. Later, we pass some delightful old houses on our right and come out to the main street of the village of Shere, which we cross to a small road opposite, leading to the church. At the end of the houses on the right, and opposite the church, we go through a gate and up a hedged path; at the end of which we turn left with a hedge on our left. Keeping on this path, along which we came earlier, we come to a lane where we turn left and out to a road.

We cross this road to take the road signposted to Dorking, turning left at the railway bridge and out to the road at Gomshall Mill. Turning right at the main road, we pass Mulligans restaurant on the left and Gomshall station is just beyond.

For the longer walk over Blackheath and Brook:

Here, we turn left on the track, keeping right when it forks almost at once. Reaching a road we cross straight over, turning immediately right at the edge of a playing field parallel with the road. We soon pass several seats and a memorial plaque which tells us 'From this spot in May 1944 Field Marshall Sir Bernard Montgomery (Monty) addressed Canadian troops prior to the D-Day landings'.

We cross a drive leading to a pavilion and, keeping the trees on our right, we take the first footpath on the right. This takes us down to a wide sandy track, up a path opposite and soon across a clearing, with buildings over on the left. (Notice the chimneys which are characteristic of the old buildings in this area.) We continue ahead along a wide bridleway, later ignoring a downhill path on the right. At a crossing path, we turn left through a plantation, emerging over a stile into a field.

We go downhill towards three or four trees and, keeping them on our right, soon cross the railway, continuing forward to a tree-lined sunken path, which bears left to an attractive timbered farmhouse. After going through gates and between farm buildings, we pass abandoned watercress beds on our right and come out to a lane, where we turn right at a fingerpost onto a sandy uphill path. Near the top we take the first track on our left, keep left at the fork and, at a crossing track, go left over a waymarked stile and along a wide track through a plantation. This ends with a stile and we go downhill over a field, later bearing slightly left to a gate and down to the road at Brook.

We turn left on the road and right into the lane to Shere and Peaslake, passing some pleasant cottages. Just before the railway bridge, which we passed near earlier in the walk, we take the signposted footpath on the right along a tarmac drive to Ponds Farm at the end. After a short enclosed path, we turn left on a crossing bridleway which later becomes tarmac and, after passing a few cottages, at the level crossing we turn right continuing past Parklands Farm. We turn left on the road and soon right on a signposted footpath between wire fences. At a wider track, we turn left and out to a road where we turn right and almost immediately left along a gravel drive. Keeping straight ahead on an enclosed grassy track, which bears right with a wall, at a crossing path we turn left across a field. Just before the hedge ahead, we fork right to the corner of the field and join a bridleway crossing the railway. We continue down to a wider lane and keep straight ahead with Old Barn on the right, bearing right out to a road. We cross the road, turn left at the railway bridge and out to the main road at Gomshall Mill, turning right at the main road, passing Mulligans restaurant on the left. Gomshall station is just beyond.

Refreshments: Gomshall Mill. There are also inns at Little London, Shere and Gomshall.

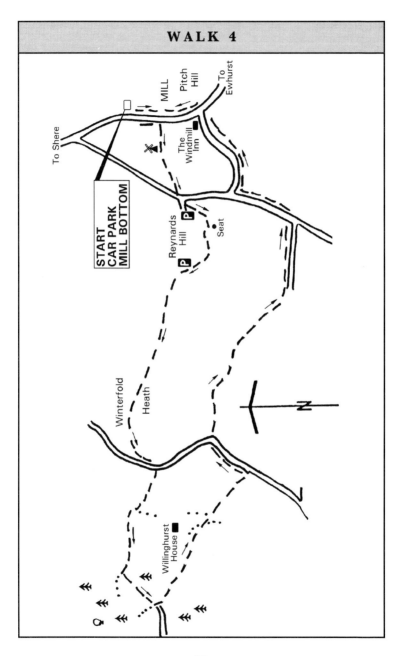

START
CAR PARK
MILL BOTTOM

To Shere

MILL

Pitch Hill

To Ewhurst

The Windmill Inn

Reynards Hill

Seat

Winterfold Heath

N

Willinghurst House

WINDMILL HILL

Reynards Hill, Winterfold Hill, Great Copse.
5½ miles

This is a walk through bilberries, pines, beeches and birches, on the less frequented hills west of Holmbury Hill and Pitch Hill, with some expansive views. Deer can frequently be seen and it is a good walk for any time of year.

How to get there: By car to Hurtwood control car park 3 at the southern end of Mill Bottom, at the foot of Pitch Hill. Turn off the A25 at Shere and the car park is 4 miles down on the left, just before reaching the Windmill Inn.

Leaving the car park, we cross the road to an uphill track at the side of Mill Cottage, avoiding a sunken path that bears right. Our path resembles a gully at first but when we have reached the top of Windmill Hill it leads us past a windmill, now used as a residence. Keeping left and, with buildings on our left, we continue downhill, over a crossing track, and reach the road at a fork. Between the forks is Hurtwood control car park 4 and from this we take a footpath leading right.

This fairly broad track leads us through woods and out to a clearing at the top of Reynards Hill, with the chance to rest on a seat provided and admire the view. Hascombe Hill can be seen on the right in the distance. Continuing on our path, we ignore a right fork and, just before the road, we take a path on the left parallel with the road which we later rejoin. Passing a sunken path, we immediately take the next path on the left going uphill through woods, later crossing a drive and, after skirting a car park, we continue later somewhat downhill and take a left fork to a junction of paths. We bear left to join the main crossing track and, after passing a seat with a view on the left, we cross the corner of a car park, turning left and later go down steps to the road.

Crossing diagonally left to a bridleway, we go forward later through a gate and over a crossing track to turn left at a signposted bridleway. After about half a mile we go over a major crossing track, bearing left, then, at a footpath sign, turn left with a wire fence. We cross a stile, continue downhill and, just before a stile, we turn sharp left on a grassy track at the side of a polytunnel. We follow the track round to the left and turn right over a stile and, at the top, bear very slightly left towards the left-hand end of a row of trees in the hedge ahead. We keep a block of saplings on our left as we go forward passing close to a standpipe tap on our left. We come out to a drive and turn left and immediately right on a track and, at a car parking area, we take the left-hand path.

We pass a stile on the right and continue to the next which takes us into a plantation of conifers, with fine views over lakes, and following the fence on our left round the top of the field, out over a stile to join a track where we turn right. We turn left before a lake and, bearing right up to join a drive, we continue between houses and out to the road where we turn left. We take the first turning on the right, signposted Alderbrook, and at a multiple fork we opt for the middle track, later ignoring a left turn, and after bends when the drive forks we continue straight ahead. The path turns right, narrows, and soon we turn left keeping to the main path. We bear right as a path joins, soon turning left on a signposted bridleway, later to turn right onto the drive of Colemans Farmhouse and eventually out to the road where we turn left uphill.

We leave the road at the second turning on the right, passing

Warren Cottage, and follow the contour track round the hills, enjoying fine views. The bridleway narrows and we join a drive to reach the road at the side of Windmill Inn. We turn left up the hill to turn right into the car park.

Refreshments: The Windmill Inn is just beyond the car park.

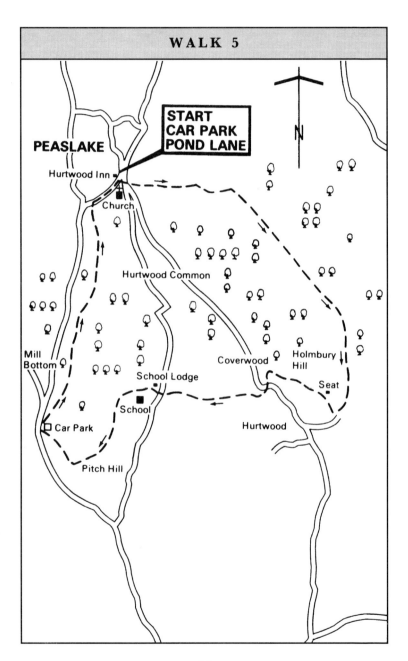

WALK 5

START
CAR PARK
POND LANE

PEASLAKE

Hurtwood Inn

Church

Hurtwood Common

Mill
Bottom

School Lodge

Coverwood

Holmbury
Hill

Seat

School

Hurtwood

Car Park

Pitch Hill

PEASLAKE

Holmbury Hill and Pitch Hill
5 miles

This walk will take us through woods, gorse and heather to Leith Hill's southerly neighbour and the wide top of Pitch Hill. From excavations in 1930, proof was obtained of a hill camp on Holmbury Hill dating from 150 BC to AD 50. The camp is now rather overgrown with brambles and bracken but can be traced round the four sides of the top. This is a wonderful walk for any time of the year, but in winter the views are enhanced by the absence of leaves and undergrowth.

How to get there: By bus from Guildford. By car to Peaslake, turning off the A25 at Gomshall. The car park is down Pond Lane next to the Hurtwood Inn.

Walking back to the inn, we turn left, then right, then left again up Radnor Road opposite the war memorial. Almost immediately there is a steep footpath on the left, but if this looks too steep, we can continue on the road and turn left along Plaws Hill which will bring us to the top of the steep path.

With Tor Cottage on our left, we go forward on a track, initially surfaced, over various crossing tracks in woods, down a dip and up the other side, soon bearing slightly right, with a field on our left. After passing a house in fields on our left, we go over a wide track and turn obliquely left for about 30 yards when we turn right on a smaller crossing track. We keep on through conifers, ignoring side turnings and soon go uphill.

Our track is now very sandy and the vegetation mainly conifers, heather and bracken. Later, we can see our track ahead dipping down to a valley and up the other side. After crossing the valley, at the top of the hill, we continue over a crossing track to a second crossing track at a small green 'triangle', where we go forward slightly left. At a major forestry track we turn right and are shortly at a junction of five paths. We take the third on the left, which is straight ahead and, as the path bears right and forks, we take the right fork.

Later, the hillside becomes fairly open, giving good views on our left. At the next fork we go left and continue round the hillside for a further half mile, keeping to the main path. We finally reach the open space and circular memorial seat at the top of Holmbury Hill.

Leaving the memorial seat on our left, we cross the open space to two paths. We take the left one and continue round the edge of the hill, ignoring three paths which successively join us on our right. The path then goes downhill and, at a fork, we turn right to a T-junction and pond, bearing left to Hurtwood control car park 1 on our right. We keep left to a narrow tarmac road, where we turn right and, after a few yards, take a path on the left, going downhill.

We turn left on a crossing track and, later, turn right round a hairpin bend and soon turn left on an enclosed path, which takes us across the valley, giving pleasant views. After half a mile, we reach the road opposite the lodge of the Duke of Kent school where the public footpath goes through the school grounds. With the lodge on our right, we follow the drive and, when it turns left towards the main school building, we continue forward uphill on a stepped path under trees, leaving the sports field on our right. We bear left uphill behind buildings then go through a gate in the perimeter fencing and up to a track, which we cross to a steep path opposite. It is possible to avoid this steep path by turning right for about 100 yards or so and, at a T-junction, turning left. After passing a footpath sign on our left, (where the steep path emerges), we continue forward and soon take a right fork. After going uphill, we turn left on a crossing track and eventually are in the open, with panoramic views and the South Downs visible on a clear day. We continue on our path, keeping to the left on the edge of the hilltop and finally turn right to the main open space of Coneyhurst or Pitch Hill with an OS trig point at a height of 843 ft. Continuing beyond the trig point on a sandy track, we later pass a quarry on our right and gradually go downhill to Hurtwood control car park 3 by the road.

We go through the car park and along the track known as Mill Bottom under trees which are mainly beech. At a fork, we keep left and maintain direction on a pleasant and easy path for over a mile until we reach Hurtwood control car park 2 which leads out to the road. Here, we turn right and, using a parallel path at a slightly higher level on the right of the road, continue into Peaslake passing the church and a small shop. The Hurtwood Inn is on our left and the car park behind it.

Refreshments: The Hurtwood Inn and the village store in Peaslake.

WALK 6

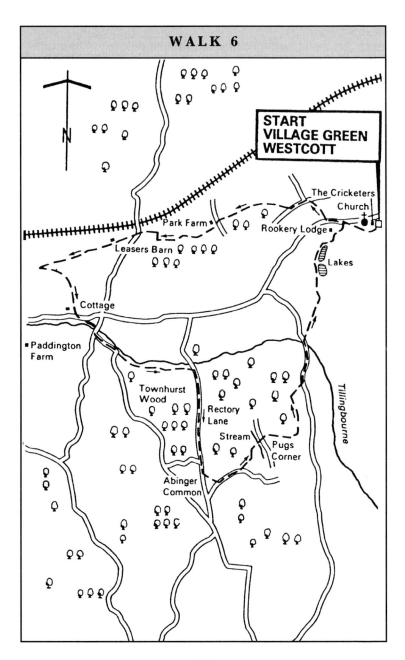

START
VILLAGE GREEN
WESTCOTT

The Cricketers
Church
Park Farm
Rookery Lodge
Leasers Barn
Lakes
Cottage
Paddington Farm
Townhurst Wood
Rectory Lane
Stream
Pugs Corner
Abinger Common
Tillingbourne

34

WESTCOTT

Broomy Down, Townhurst Wood, The Rookery
6³/₄ miles

This is an interesting walk over heathland and through woodland where deer abound. It affords delightful views across the valley and is pleasant at any time of year.

How to get there: There is a bus service from Dorking to Westcott which is about 2 miles from the centre of Dorking. Cars can be parked in the side road leading from the Cricketers pub up to Westcott church.

From the triangular village green at Westcott, we continue along the main road for a few yards to the Cricketers, where we turn left. Just past the church and opposite the cemetery on the left, we take a wide path on the right leading us over a grassy area in front of a few houses. We cross a small drive leading to the houses and go forward to the centre one of three paths. We maintain direction slightly downhill. Our path becomes gully-like, with orange-coloured sandhills on the right, and we are soon out to the main road by Rookery Lodge.

We cross the main road turning left, continue past Balchins Lane and turn right up Coast Hill Lane, which almost immediately turns left while we continue forward on an enclosed footpath between gardens. We are soon walking on a fenced path in an area of holly, beech and conifer trees and, after bearing left and slightly downhill, we are out on a small tarmac drive. Here we turn left onto a farm track bounded by fields, keeping right when it forks. We proceed through trees on a wide track, pass a red-brick house and continue to Park Farm.

With the farmhouse on the right, we go forward, with farm buildings either side. We keep on this track with Deerleap Woods on the left and open fields on the right, enjoying pleasant views across the valley to White Downs. After about half a mile, we are out in the road which leads from Effingham to the A25. We turn left, then almost immediately right, on a well-defined path, later passing the Bishop Wilberforce monument which marks the spot where he was thrown from his horse and killed in 1873, and Leasers Barn. We continue uphill through woodland, on a wide gravel track. Immediately on reaching the open area of Broomy Down, we turn left off the path, pass two pine trees and before reaching the far side of the clearing, we turn left by a waymarked post onto a grassy ride, shortly bearing right, going over a crossing track to a stile and open field. We go forward, passing some isolated trees on our left, then cross a stile in the left-hand corner to a path, with the walled courtyard of the stable block of former Abinger Hall on our right. This path has been planted with bulbs for the enjoyment of walkers.

Our path comes out to the main road which we cross to a stile opposite and, going diagonally across a field to a stile, we come out to a secondary road where we turn right and then shortly left into a smaller road. We pass Abinger Mill House on the left and go over a stile to a path into a wood, with a stream on our left. We remain on this path through Townhurst Wood for over half a mile. Deer may be seen here if we are quiet.

On reaching a road, Rectory Lane, we turn right and remain on this road for almost half a mile. About 150 yards past a road on the right, and just past some wooden gateposts at the side of the road, we take a footpath on our left, continuing forward over a crossing track and keeping left at a fork. Our path bears left and is soon parallel with a small road on our right. At a farm track, we join the road and then turn left down a private drive which ends at a house where we turn right, crossing a stream by a bridge, and go over a stile to a small path opposite, climbing steeply uphill. After the path flattens, we continue between woods and young tree plantations, later turning left with the path and left again at a junction of paths. Our track turns right and soon goes downhill; bears left and becomes parallel, with a sunken road on our right.

We eventually come out over a stile to the road, where we turn left, and, after crossing the Tillingbourne, we turn right, going uphill into trees and emerging onto a private drive. The footpath crosses the drive diagonally up a steep bank, and through trees to a bridleway where we turn left towards a house.

We pass the house on our left, going through brick gateposts and turning right. At the end of the path, we bear right alongside a wide track and immediately turn left over a stile. This path takes us steeply downhill to a wider bridleway where we maintain direction, passing a lake on our right and going through the Rookery on the main drive, later past several delightful houses. We finally reach the road with the Rookery Lodge on our left and turn right on a footpath parallel with the road past the sandhills on our left. We keep forward on the main path crossing the drive and the open space in front of houses, finally coming out to the road by the cemetery where we turn left down to Westcott church where the walk began.

Refreshments: Inns and shops at Westcott.

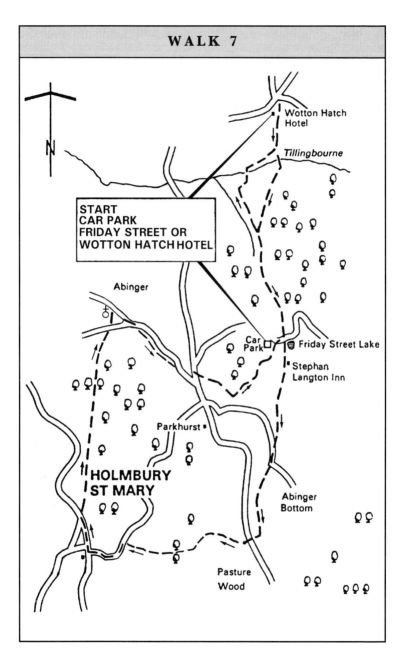

START
CAR PARK
FRIDAY STREET OR
WOTTON HATCH HOTEL

Wotton Hatch Hotel

Tillingbourne

Abinger

Car Park

Friday Street Lake

Stephan Langton Inn

Parkhurst

HOLMBURY ST MARY

Abinger Bottom

Pasture Wood

FRIDAY STREET

Abinger Bottom, Holmbury St Mary, Pasture Wood, Abinger, and back to Friday Street.
5 mile circular walk from Friday Street car park, but, if done from Wotton Hatch Hotel, 7$^{1}/_{2}$ miles

This is a woodland walk for any time of the year, with bluebells, rhododendrons and foxgloves in season and deer to be seen by the quiet observer.

How to get there: By car to Friday Street. The car park is 200 yards west on the Abinger Road. By bus to Wotton Hatch.

Starting from Friday Street car park:

With the car park behind us and, facing the road, we turn right onto a narrow path parallel with the road, but at a higher level, following it to some wooden steps, which we go down, turning left into the road and right to Friday Street lake.

From Wotton Hatch Hotel to Friday Street (just under 1$^{1}/_{4}$ miles):

Leaving the hotel on our right, we take the drive to a gate at the side of a wooden building, go over a stile and diagonally right across a field to the far corner. (NB **not** over a stile in the fence on the right.) We continue over another stile, down through a strip of woodland, and over a meadow, crossing the

Tillingbourne. Our path then takes us up towards a wood and over a stile bearing right uphill through woods. After crossing a wider track, we maintain direction for about half a mile, with a wire fence on the right, going uphill and later downhill to ponds and a stream in the valley. We turn left at this T-junction and follow the track for about half a mile, crossing a stile with a bridge and pond on the right. We then continue on the wide bridleway, pass a couple of cottages, and come out to the lake at Friday Street.

With the lake on our left, we walk along the little road passing the Stephan Langton Inn and, when it ends, we keep straight ahead on a footpath for about half a mile when it joins a tarmac lane. We turn left into Abinger Bottom and, as the lane turns left, we keep straight ahead on a path through open woods. At a crossing path with a waymarked post, we turn right uphill to a minor road where we turn left. Almost immediately there is a track on the right leading to a junction of paths and a signpost.

We continue straight ahead on the signposted footpath along an enclosed path for a short distance, with a field on our left. A stile takes us into open meadows and we maintain direction, soon with a hedge on our left. At the end of the field, we go through a gate and stile on the right to a crossing track where we turn left and almost immediately right on a waymarked path. This path twists and turns but is very well waymarked. We continue through open woodland and, just after passing a large field on the right, with a house visible ahead, we turn sharply left on a waymarked track. We follow this pleasant path and later cross a wide grassy forestry track to continue on a narrower path down to a road where we turn left down to the main road.

We turn right through Holmbury St Mary passing the Holly Bush Tavern on our left. At an old village pump, we turn right on a gravel drive, go through a gate and just past the lodge keep left at a fork. We follow this main track for nearly half a mile. A wide track on the left leads to the road and we continue forward over a stile beside a gate into a wide track, soon with a field on our left. The track goes very gradually uphill and later we ignore a right turning and bear slightly left. When this path forks, we take the left fork which goes more steeply uphill eventually reaching a stile taking us into a meadow. This we cross to a stile in the hedge ahead, going down steps to a small road, where we turn right. On the left is the village green where, on the second Saturday in June, the annual Medieval Fair is held. There is also a seat, the church and Abinger Hatch Hotel to the right.

We follow the road to the T-junction and turn right through the village of Abinger, passing some pleasant houses and a small housing estate. Just past the last house on the left in the village, we turn left on a signposted gravel path, with a green on the right. At a gate, we take the right fork to a small road which we cross to a footpath opposite, taking us into woods, soon ignoring a left fork. After about half a mile, when the path is much wider, we turn left at a crossing track. We pass another crossing track and, on reaching a junction of five paths, we take the second on the left, shortly keeping left at a fork and eventually coming to the car park.

To return to Wotton Hatch Hotel, we turn right on the road to Friday Street lake and turn left onto the bridleway along which we came. We keep on this for just over half a mile but, instead of turning right on the path we used at the beginning of the walk, we keep straight on. The track goes downhill and we turn right on a crossing track and immediately left down to a stile by a stream, then up a field ahead to a stile where we turn right on a drive. After 200 yards or so we cross a stile in the fence on our right and return over the field to Wotton Hatch Hotel.

Refreshments: Inns at Holmbury St Mary and Abinger, the Stephan Langton at Friday Street and Wotton Hatch Hotel.

WALK 8

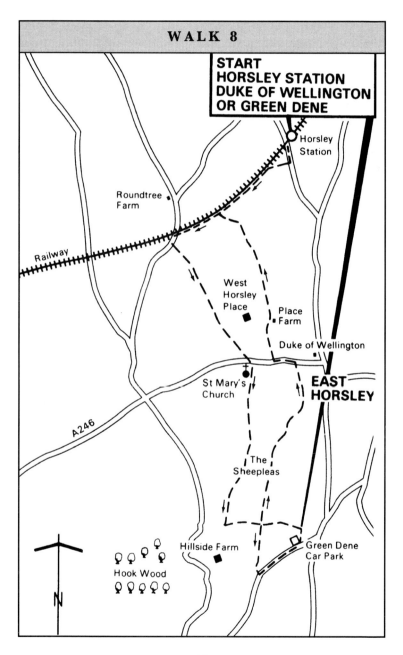

**START
HORSLEY STATION
DUKE OF WELLINGTON
OR GREEN DENE**

Horsley
Station

Roundtree
Farm

Railway

West
Horsley
Place

Place
Farm

Duke of Wellington

St Mary's
Church

**EAST
HORSLEY**

The
Sheepleas

A246

Hillside Farm

Green Dene
Car Park

Hook Wood

N

HORSLEY

**Sheepleas
5 miles**

In late spring and early summer, the open area of Sheepleas supports an abundance of wild flowers and several species of orchid. There are also copious amounts of deadly nightshade. This bushy plant has purple bell-shaped flowers, followed by shiny black berries resembling cherries, and children should be warned not to touch them.

Walks 8 and 9 form a figure of eight and if a 10 mile walk is desired, instead of turning left for the car park, we cross the road to a signposted bridleway into Mountain Wood and follow walk 9.

How to get there: By train to Horsley railway station. By bus to the Duke of Wellington pub at East Horsley. By car on the A246 from Leatherhead to Guildford, turning on the signposted road to Green Dene and Sheepleas a third of a mile east of East Horsley, continuing down the road for $1\frac{1}{2}$ miles to the car park on the right.

If using the bus to the *Duke of Wellington*:

Walk towards Guildford for about a quarter of a mile and take the bridleway on the right to Place Farm and continue the walk from (**A**).

If starting from Horsley station:

Turn right down the approach road, crossing the main road to take the small road by the side of a hotel, keeping parallel with the railway on the right. This soon becomes a footpath alongside the railway and eventually comes out to the road. Now continue the walk from (**B**).

Starting from the car park in Green Dene:

With our backs to the road, we take a path at the right-hand corner of the car park and turn right, initially parallel with the road. In about a quarter of a mile, we cross an avenue of yew trees and continue forward uphill to a wider crossing track where we turn left. After about 200 yards or so, we cross a track and continue forward across an open area and, at a junction of paths, take the first turning on the right downhill.

At the next junction of paths we continue forward i.e. the second on the right. We continue downhill to a major crossing track where we turn right into a tree-lined track soon with fields on our left. St Mary's church, West Horsley, is soon visible in the distant trees on our left. When we come to the road, we turn left and soon take a bridleway on the right to Place Farm.

(**A**) Immediately after the farmhouse, we turn right following the bridleway sign to a track, later hedged, and then across open fields then through woods eventually coming to the railway line. (To return to the station, we turn right.)

We turn left and follow the path alongside the railway line until it comes out to a road.

(**B**) We turn left and, in a few yards, go over a stile in the hedge on our left. Keeping the hedge on our left, we continue to a signpost beside a stile and turn right round the next field to a gap and stile in the hedge. Continuing with the hedge on our left, we come out opposite St Mary's church, West Horsley.

Crossing the main road, we take the bridleway with the church on our right.

This church is well worth a visit and much of it is very old. There is a fragment of Saxon stonework and Late Norman pillars and arches; the tower doorway is also Late Norman. A 12th century wall painting depicts St Christopher, the patron saint of travellers, and pilgrims' crosses can be seen on the arch of the 12th century north doorway.

Keeping the trees on our right, at the end of the field on our left, we continue direction through a gate into an open area with trees on our right. The path continues through a strip of wood and across the centre of another open area going slightly uphill to a seat. We turn right on a crossing track and almost at once, at a junction of paths, take the second on the right signposted to Shere Road car park. A barrier gives access to a path into a third open area. There is a waymarked post on the left where we fork right up a slope passing a seat to the right soon finding the stone cairn of the Millennium viewpoint. From here we bear right to a track and turn left and left again, with an open space and picnic tables on our right, and at the corner of the open space turn right with trees still on our left. The path goes through a strip of woodland to reach a main bridleway where we turn left, soon taking a right fork. As the track curves left, there is a waymarked post and we turn right on a grass path which bears right through some trees to reach a gate into a field where we turn left. Leaving the field by another gate, we turn right and right again on a wide track with a marker post. Later we turn left on a smaller path passing a waymark and continuing downhill turning right at a junction, then straight ahead to Green Dene car park.

If we want the longer walk through Mountain Wood, we do not take the smaller path but continue downhill to the road on the wider bridleway.

Refreshments: The Duke of Wellington on the A246.

WALK 9

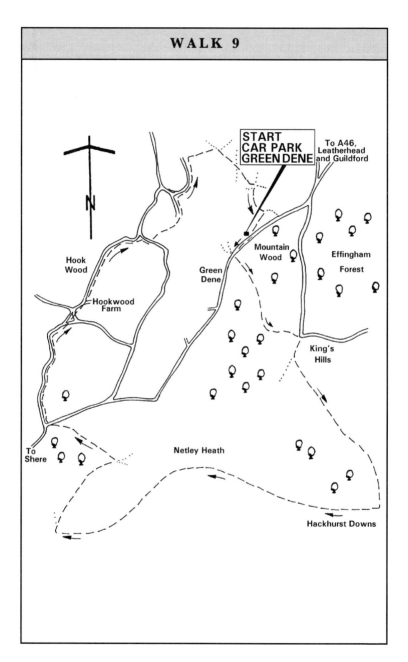

START CAR PARK GREEN DENE

To A46, Leatherhead and Guildford

Hook Wood

Hookwood Farm

Green Dene

Mountain Wood

Effingham Forest

King's Hills

To Shere

Netley Heath

Hackhurst Downs

MOUNTAIN WOOD

**Netley Heath, 5³/₄ miles
A circular walk from the car park
in Green Dene through woodland.**

This is a lovely walk for all seasons but is particularly recommended for the autumn when the larches of Netley Heath are turning yellow. There are many different types of fungi to be seen on this walk, and blackberries and sweet chestnuts for the gathering.

How to get there: By car on the A246 Leatherhead to Guildford road, turning left on the signposted road to Green Dene and Sheepleas a third of a mile east of East Horsley, continuing down the road for 1¹/₂ miles to the car park on the right.

From the car park, we turn right along the road for a short distance and, just before a house on the right, we turn left, on a signposted bridleway, into Mountain Wood. We keep on the main track for about half a mile, which later drops very steeply down to a wide forestry road where we turn right to go through a gateway and log stacking area. At a broken down gate, marking the entrance to a lumber works, we turn left on a track through trees. Ignoring side turnings we continue for about three-quarters of a mile, and as the track bears left, we maintain direction on a smaller path.

We finally turn right on a droveway, soon ignoring the main

track as it turns left, and continue ahead past metal gates and, after a quarter of a mile, turn left to the open space of Hackhurst Downs. As we go forward, with an information board and seat on our right, we ignore a left turn. We follow the path round to rejoin the droveway and shortly come to a viewpoint and seat. We continue on this droveway for just over 1 mile and at a junction of paths, with a water reservoir over to the left, we turn right, soon ignoring a left fork, and continue through open woodland until, at a junction of paths, we turn left on a bridleway.

We go forward through the car park at Francis Corner to the road where we turn left and shortly right on an enclosed bridleway later between fields and emerging to cross over a track to a drive between houses. Taking the left fork to an enclosed bridleway we soon pass Hookwood and, after about a quarter of a mile, we cross a concrete yard turning right and then left to follow the drive down to the road. We turn right for a short distance then turn left on a track taking us between farm buildings until at a crossing drive we turn left enjoying the fine views.

When the field on the right ends, we take a path on the right along the edge and at a gate on the right we turn left on a bridleway out into the open. We turn left at a T-junction, going gently downhill and, at a waymark post on the left, we turn right soon to take the left fork. We bear right at a T-junction and again bear right at the next to continue gently uphill ignoring side turnings. A main path joins from the left and we immediately fork left to maintain direction on a main bridleway, later bearing left to a junction of paths with a waymark. We take the second path on the left, going gently downhill into woods. After about 150 yards, with a large yew tree on our right, we turn right onto a small path which weaves its way downhill and finally reaches the car park.

RANMORE

Effingham Golf Course and Polesden Lacey
5 miles

This is a varied walk of woods and fields in a little known area, with changing views. It is lovely in the spring and autumn while the bare trees of winter open up the viewpoints still further.

How to get there: By car on the A24 from London, turning off for Guildford just before Dorking station (Ashcombe Road), turning right again for Ranmore. Stoneyrock Road is the second turning on the right about 3 miles from Dorking station, and there is a car park on the left, just before a cottage.

Just before the cottage, we turn left on a track and continue between fields on a fenced path which is rather muddy during wet weather. After going down a dip, with a house on the left, we go up to a road.

We cross the road to a gravelled drive ahead and, as this bears right, we cross a stile, maintain our direction, then go over two stiles and straight down the field to a road which we cross diagonally right to a footpath. We go straight up through a wood with fields on the right, over a couple of stiles and, at the waymarked second stile, turn right through a strip of wood to another stile and a footpath sign. Turning left with a wire fence

WALK 10

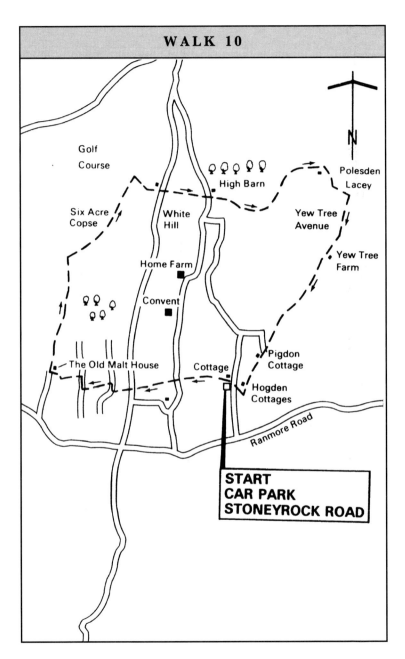

Golf Course

Six Acre Copse

High Barn

Polesden Lacey

White Hill

Yew Tree Avenue

Home Farm

Yew Tree Farm

Convent

The Old Malt House

Cottage

Pigdon Cottage

Hogden Cottages

Ranmore Road

START
CAR PARK
STONEYROCK ROAD

on our left we go through a field to a gate and stile onto a wide bridleway.

Here we turn right and very soon left over a signposted stile, along the side of a field, bearing right to a stile, then through a wood down to a beautiful timbered house, The Old Malt House, which we keep on our right, turning right into a bridleway. We follow the bridleway for about a quarter of a mile and at a house turn right on a path through woods, keeping left at a way post, following it for half a mile. A stile takes us into a sloping field and we continue along the top edge to the corner when we cross another stile back into the woods. Bearing right we continue direction through Six Acre Copse, eventually coming out to Effingham golf course.

Maintaining our direction, we cross the golf course to the left-hand end of a clump of trees round which we turn right. There is an electricity hut half hidden in the trees on the right and we cross another fairway making for the left-hand of a small copse with a garden hedge on the left. A grassy track, with the grounds of a large house on our left, brings us out to a road which we cross to a track opposite. Bearing left, then right, we go through a gate into a large field and, with the hedge on our right, follow this track to another road.

We turn right for a few yards then left beside buildings which we keep on our left and continue on a path for a quarter of a mile on the edge of woods to a junction of paths. Here we turn left through a gate on a path through trees, following it for half a mile. We then have a field on our left and our path bears right until finally there are trees on our left and an open field on our right. We continue over a crossing track and bear right round a field towards buildings on the Polesden Lacey estate. At a drive we turn right to go under a thatched bridge, passing on our left the date (1861) marked in the flintstone embankment. When the drive turns left, we continue ahead down a spectacular avenue of yew trees and when it joins another track we bear right, passing Yew Tree Farm on our left and ignoring a path forking off to the right.

Shortly after passing the farm we turn right into a field through a waymarked gate. We keep along the top edge of this field with the woods on our left and lovely views across the valley. At the brick remains of a cattle trough we bear diagonally right down a sloping field to a stile in the hedge which brings us into a track bounded by a flint wall.

Here, we turn left and go straight ahead passing Pigdon on our right. After the next building, Hogden Cottage, we turn right uphill on a track with a 'No Horses' sign and with the cottage gardens on our right finally come out to the road and the car park.

RANMORE AND POLESDEN LACEY

From Boxhill station through the woods of Ranmore and Polesden Lacey (a National Trust property).
6½ miles

A zigzag walk in the lovely woods of Ranmore Common, with many outstanding views. In season there are bluebells, foxgloves, orchids and, if we are quiet, deer. It is recommended for any time of the year.

How to get there: By train to Boxhill railway station. There is a small car park at the station. Bus or Green Line coach to Burford Bridge Hotel on the A24 where there is a free car park opposite the hotel. Motorists should leave the A24 at a turning signposted West Humble.

Leaving Boxhill station, we go up the steps and turn left over the bridge taking the left fork, Chapel Lane. We stay on the road for half a mile but there is a parallel footpath on the left for some of the way. Passing Burney Road and the last of the houses on our left, we take a footpath diagonally between wire fences across a field to a T-junction where we turn left. The remains of an ancient chapel can be seen away on our right. We continue along this tree fringed bridleway. Just underneath the pylon lines we take a right fork and after a few yards go over a stile on the right, keeping parallel with the power

WALK 11

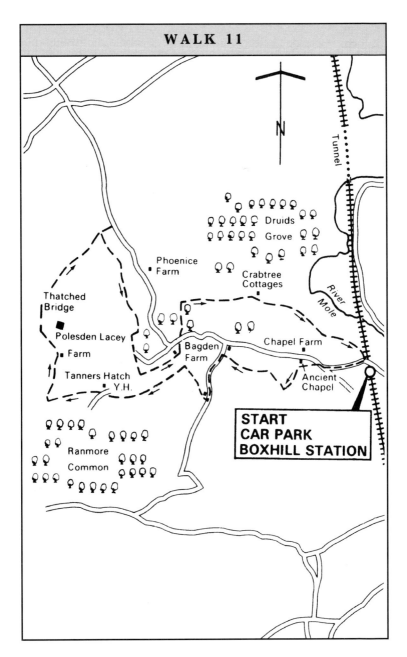

Druids Grove

Phoenice Farm

Crabtree Cottages

Thatched Bridge

Polesden Lacey Farm

Bagden Farm

Chapel Farm

Tanners Hatch Y.H.

Ancient Chapel

Ranmore Common

START CAR PARK BOXHILL STATION

Tunnel

River Mole

cables to another stile. Keeping along this path with a wire fence and open fields on our right and a sloping wood on the left, we go over a stile and along a hedge on our right to a cottage and a road. Here we turn left and after a quarter of a mile we pass a cottage on the right, then an open field, soon coming to a wood where we turn right going uphill. Reaching the top of the hill, at a T-junction, we turn right, soon going slightly downhill. At the end of the wood the path turns left downhill, and as the path turns right we turn left through a gate over a field and shortly enter woods ignoring a left turning. Soon we take a left fork and almost immediately a right fork going uphill. Later, at another fork we keep right and finally bear right downhill to Tanners Hatch Youth Hostel.

We turn left and keep right into woods which later give way to open fields on the right beyond which Polesden Lacey can be seen. We follow this path uphill, keeping forward to a bridleway and a cottage where we turn right downhill, passing Polesden farmbuildings at the bottom, then uphill again along a drive. At the top, we turn right with the drive, soon going under a small thatched bridge. After the bridge the sharp-eyed may be able to spot the date 1861 in dressed flints in the flintstone embankment on the right. Turning right with the drive, which soon becomes a stony track between fields, we pass the entrance to Polesden Lacey on our right, the house and gardens of which are well worth a visit.

To continue the walk, we follow the drive for another quarter of a mile, using a path along the verge on the right. After going slightly uphill to a line of trees on our right, we turn right on a bridleway for about three quarters of a mile when it turns right into woods and soon bears left downhill. We go under a bridge and continue to the bottom of the hill where the bridleway bears right, while we turn left at a gate and cross a field on a well defined path. With Bagden Farm on our left, we turn left on a crossing track and are soon at the road.

We cross to a bridleway opposite, soon going through a gate and uphill into woods, later continuing diagonally right over a field. After a quarter of a mile, at the top of the hill, with a stile and open fields on the left, we turn right on a path through trees. Its twists and turns can be followed until we come to an open field on our right giving us views of Ranmore church. We are soon out to Crabtree Cottages and a lane where we turn right for about 1 mile to Boxhill station.

Refreshments: Polesden Lacey tea rooms in the summer. Refreshment van at Burford Bridge car park.

DORKING

**Deepdene, Betchworth golf course, Glory Wood.
6 miles**

This is a pleasant walk in woods and over farmland, keeping quite close to Dorking but giving views of the hills we have visited on other walks in this book. A little mud will be encountered in winter but in April and May the larch woods near the Betchworth golf course are turning green and there are bluebells in the woods.

How to get there: By train or bus to Dorking railway station where there is a car park.

From Dorking station approach road, we take the subway under the road and turn right (south). After going under the railway bridge we take the first turning on the right, following it to the main road where we cross to Moores Road. This soon forks and we keep right, going uphill to the open green of Cotmandene, forward towards trees, then down to Chart Lane where we continue direction.

Chart Lane joins the main road (A24), which we cross, bearing slightly left to a signposted footpath leading up to Deepdene. We are soon walking parallel with the main road

WALK 12

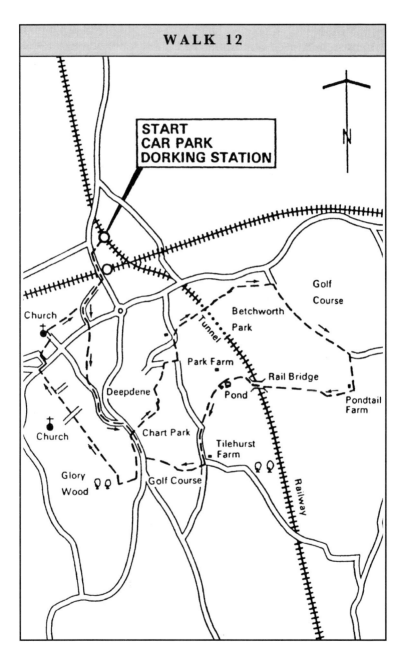

START
CAR PARK
DORKING STATION

Golf
Course

Betchworth
Park

Church

Tunnel

Park Farm

Rail Bridge

Deepdene

Pond

Pondtail
Farm

Church

Chart Park

Tilehurst
Farm

Glory
Wood

Golf Course

Railway

among rhododendron thickets. When the track turns right, we turn sharply left and still uphill with occasional wooden steps in the steepest parts. At the top, we bear slightly left and as we proceed along the now flat path there are good views to be had on the right over the golf course and beyond.

Soon our path leads us to a tarmac drive where we turn left, continuing between the houses and gardens of the Deepdene estate. We turn right at a T-junction, finally bearing right and out to a road, Punchbowl Lane, where we turn left. After just over 100 yards, we turn right along a tarmac drive and, when this turns right, we leave the drive by a footpath on the left under larch trees.

We eventually pass the rear of the clubhouse on our right and continue down to a drive which we cross diagonally right to a gate and fenced track across the golf course. After about half a mile we turn right on a signposted footpath with a pond on our right, keeping to the edge of fields with a hedge and ditch on our right making for Pondtail Farm. We cross the farm track into a field, where after a few yards we turn right over a plank bridge and stile, going forward along the edge of the field with a hedge and a small stream on our right. At the end of the next field, we go over a stile into a narrow belt of conifers, then turn right and immediately left on a track at the edge of a field with a ditch and conifers on our left.

After about a quarter of a mile, we go under a railway bridge and across a field on a wide grassy track leading towards Park Farm. The track takes us past a pond with farm buildings on our left and the main farmhouse uphill on the right. We do not go over the cattle grid but turn left on another track, with trees on our right and fields on our left. We pass cottages on our right and finally go downhill to a road where we turn left.

When Tilehurst Lane turns off on our left, we turn right on a grassy track, which leads across the golf course, uphill through woods and finally out to the main road (A24). We turn right and after about 150 yards, just before Chart Lane turns off, we cross to the other side of the road and take a small doubling-back path between hedges. We soon have a field on our right and on our left, screened by trees, a deep drop down to the main road. Our path bears right into open woodland, known as Glory Wood, and we continue uphill under trees with a good view of Dorking on our right.

At the end of the open space on our right the path re-enters woods and we are soon at a T-junction where we turn right, past seats and an information board, along a main track through Glory Wood.

Leaving the wood we keep right downhill to pass between school buildings and continue direction on a path between houses and gardens. After passing a flintstone wall on our left, we go down some steps, cross a road leading to a car park, downhill at the side of Chequers Yard and out into the main street of Dorking.

Here we turn right, cross over the pedestrian crossing, and turn left down Mill Lane. We pass the Malt House and turn right in a park following the Pipp Brook out to a road where we turn left down to the main road. We turn left, go under the railway bridge and under the subway, to Dorking station.

Refreshments: Teashops and inns in Dorking.

LEITH HILL

The eastern slopes of Leith Hill, Redlands, Anstiebury Farm, Kitlands
6 miles

This is an exhilarating and rather hilly walk, with magnificent views on paths amid deer country, far from the throng of people. Concentration is necessary as we twist and turn among heather and trees.

How to get there; By car from Dorking on the Coldharbour Road to a car park at the Landslip just south of Coldharbour village and just beyond the bend sign in the road. By bus or train to Holmwood railway station.

The walk starts from the car park at the Landslip but **if starting from Holmwood Station** turn to (**3**).

From the car park between the road on the left and a high slope on the right ,we follow a clear path signed to the Tower. We join a main track coming up from the road and turn right uphill through conifers which later give way to beech trees. At the top, we go through a barrier downhill on a main track which is joined by another from the right and proceeds to a crossing track with a deep gully on our left known as Cockshot Hollow. The main path on the left goes up to the tower at the top of Leith Hill.

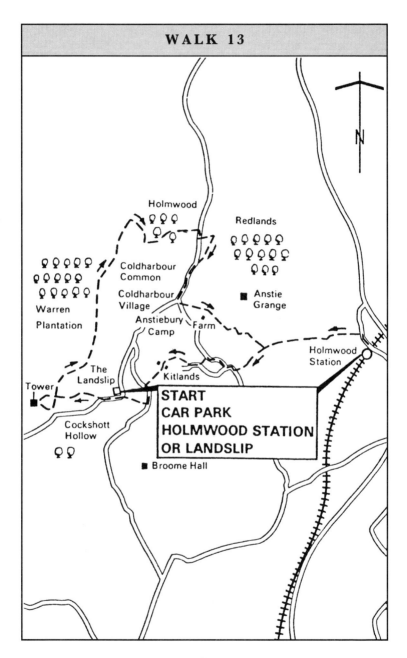

Holmwood

Redlands

Coldharbour
Common

Warren

Plantation

Coldharbour
Village

Anstie
Grange

Anstiebury
Camp

Farm

Holmwood
Station

Tower

The
Landslip

Kitlands

**START
CAR PARK
HOLMWOOD STATION
OR LANDSLIP**

Cockshott
Hollow

Broome Hall

N

The top of Leith Hill is 965 ft but a height of over 1,000 ft can be attained from the tower which was originally built by Richard Hull of Leith Hill Place in 1766. He died in 1772 and by his wish was buried in the tower. The tower fell into decay but was restored in 1795. At some later period a turret was added giving access to the roof. It is said that thirteen counties may be seen from the top on a very clear day.

We retrace our steps back to the top of Cockshot Hollow and cross over to the path with the National Trust sign (Dukes Warren). At a crossing track we turn left and joining the main path we turn left and, in less than 100 yards, where two paths turn off on the left, we take the second left one with larch trees on the left.

We continue for about half a mile to the second and more major waymarked crossing track on which we turn right. Later, at a junction of paths, we take the second on the left, a small uphill path through trees and after about 150 yards bear left skirting a holly bush and over a small bank to resume direction on a wide track. We eventually come out to a broad sandy track.

The walk can be shortened here by turning right along the wide track for nearly half a mile until it comes out at Coldharbour village where we turn right for just over half a mile to the car park.

To continue the walk, we turn left and at a junction of paths take a well-defined track downhill on the right. Crossing a wide forestry road we go down the path opposite to a crossing track with Lower Meridan Farm on the left where we turn right. Soon at a crossing track we go left downhill. Later we cross a small stream and soon at a junction of paths take the second left path uphill. At the top of the hill we go over a crossing track and bear right. We go forward slightly right and continue along this rather obscure path to the road where we turn right. Shortly we turn left on a tarmac track into Redlands Wood and almost at once, at a barrier, take a small uphill path on the right. At the top we turn right along a path and eventually come out to a road where we turn left.

At the road junction, the walk can be shortened by keeping

straight ahead through Coldharbour village and back to the car park. There is an inn; and confectionery and ice cream can be obtained in the village.

At the road junction we turn left and shortly turn left along the fenced path to Anstiebury Farm. Just beyond the farm buildings we take a stile on the right and go across a field to the far corner where there is another stile leading into woods. The path goes downhill, soon with a wire fence on our left, down to another stile and out into a field. We cross the field slightly left to a large oak tree, bear right with the hedge on our left down to a stile into a tree-lined track.

For Holmwood Station:

We turn left and continue back the way we came, going through the kissing gate into the enclosed path which brings us back to the road, station and bus stop.

To continue the walk back to the Landslip:

After crossing the stile into the track we turn right and follow it until it comes out to a road in which we turn right passing the lodge of Kitlands on the left.

(**2**) Just before a house on the right we turn left over a stile. Passing under telegraph wires, we keep along the edge of a field with the hedge on the right, over another stile and out to a lane where we turn right. Ignoring left forks we continue forward and later, with a wall on our left, we take a left fork. Soon this track becomes tarmac and later we go through an avenue of cypress trees and out to a road where we turn left, noticing fine views on the left before the road becomes tree lined. After about 100 yards, just before a signposted stile on the left, we turn right opposite a post then continue uphill. Eventually the path leads us out to a road and through posts where we turn left to the car park on our right.

(3) If starting from Holmwood station:

We turn left at the road for a short distance towards Dorking. At the last house on the left and at the 30 mph sign we turn left through a kissing gate along an enclosed path and out to a lane where we turn left. After just over a quarter of a mile we take the middle of three tracks. We follow this for nearly half a mile, finally bearing right out to the road where we turn right, soon passing the lodge of Kitlands on the left. Now continue at **(2)**.

Refreshments: Available from Leith Hill tower on most weekends and fine days and at Coldharbour village where there is an inn and general stores.

WALK 14

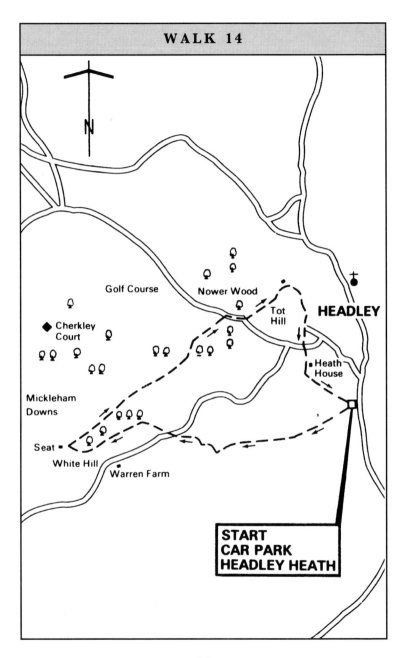

Golf Course

Nower Wood

Tot
Hill

HEADLEY

◆ Cherkley
Court

Heath
House

Mickleham
Downs

Seat ▪

White Hill

Warren Farm

**START
CAR PARK
HEADLEY HEATH**

HEADLEY HEATH

Mickleham Downs
5 miles

Here are two walks from the car park on Headley Heath: the first walking over the heath and Mickleham Downs, mostly on National Trust land; the other (Walk 15) over fields to Headley church, returning over the heath. Both walks are pleasant with bluebells in April and May and heather in August. Both are recommended for any time of the year.

How to get there: By bus from Leatherhead. By car on the B2033.

At the mobile canteen by the car park, with the road behind us, we go forward over an open space, cross a main horse track and continue on a wide path ignoring side turnings. After bearing left then right, the path bears left to a wider gravel track, soon becoming grassy, leading to a junction of five or six paths with a seat on the left and a gravel hump ahead. We take the second path on the right and very soon, at a crossing track, turn left. We have fine views on the right and reach an open space with a National Trust marker post and seat on our right. Here we turn left downhill on a stepped path. Reaching a bridleway at the bottom we turn right and take the first turning on the right winding steeply uphill. At the top we turn right with the boundary wall of former Wentworth Hall on our left. This path bears right and downhill, eventually coming out to Lodgebottom Road, with a cottage on the left.

Crossing to a footpath opposite, we take the lower path at first parallel with the road. After about 300 yards we fork left uphill under yew trees. The woods here are a mixture of very fine beech and yew trees with an underplanting of box. After a further half mile we emerge into open scrubland with a seat on the right and fine views of the northern slopes of Boxhill and Ranmore church and common. We turn right just before the seat, soon turning left at an old iron fence post. After about 20 yards, we pass a second iron fence post on our left and continue for a few yards before our path turns right. We ignore a left turning and keep right maintaining direction through a more open area eventually reaching a wide grassy ride along the top of Mickleham Downs. Here we turn right and continue for about half a mile, in summer through an abundance of wild flowers.

At the end of the ride, we continue forward into woods keeping along the fenced path with Surrey Wildlife Trust Nature Reserve on our right, eventually coming out through posts to a road. Here we turn right on a track parallel with the road and at the end cross to a bridleway opposite. Very soon we go over a stile on the right into a field with a wood on the left, bearing left round the edge of the wood. When the wood turns sharply left, we keep straight on to a stile ahead, down a field with wire fencing on the left, over another stile, passing a house on the left, and over yet another stile in the left hand corner into a lane, in which we turn right. The lane comes to a road and we again turn right passing a farm on the right. We keep straight on, ignoring a left fork.

We are shortly at a road which we cross over to the National Trust sign and take the left hand of two paths, uphill onto Headley Heath. Later, we have the thick holly hedge of Heath House on our left and, as this ends, we cross a small tarmac drive and continue on the grassy path maintaining the same direction. Our path soon bears slightly left in an open area and in sight of the road ahead we bear right to the car park.

Refreshments: Available from the mobile refreshment van at Headley Heath car park and at the Cock in Headley village. There is also a tearoom just past the Cock on the left.

WALK 15

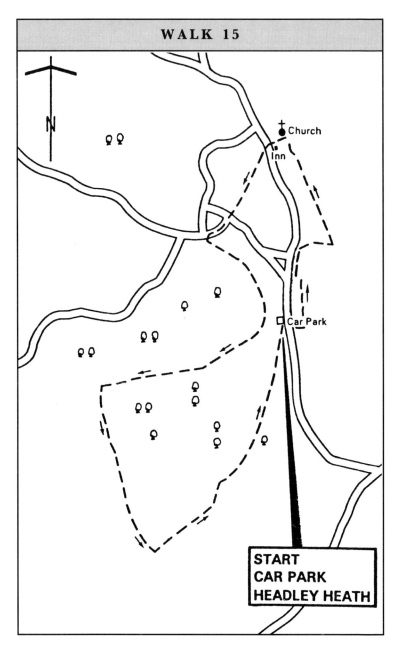

Church

Inn

Car Park

**START
CAR PARK
HEADLEY HEATH**

HEADLEY AND HEADLEY HEATH

5 miles

This walk includes some field walking but it is mainly in the woods and heathland of Headley Heath. There are Highland cattle grazing on several parts of the Headley Heath but all paths are open to the public and gates are provided for access. As the fencing is movable, we do not mention going through gates but there should be no difficulty following the route.

This walk starts from the main Headley Heath car park, free to National Trust members, opposite the cricket ground.

We cross the road to a wide grass path at the side of the cricket field and, keeping this on our left, we soon pass in front of the pavilion and bear right to reach a road where we turn left. As the road turns left we continue straight ahead through a barrier into trees and follow a small path parallel with the road. After the path becomes surfaced we maintain direction to take the right fork down a gravel drive, go over a stile on our left to continue on a footpath with a house on the right.

At a footpath sign we turn left over a field to a gate and maintain direction over various stiles until we reach Headley church. We turn left through the churchyard and reach the road, with the Cock Horse inn on our left, crossing diagonally left to the bus stop.

Here we turn right on a surfaced path which soon gives pleasant views. Reaching the road, we turn immediately right, soon keeping right at a road junction. After about 20 yards, opposite the first house, we turn left and immediately fork right on a path through woods, Tot Hill, a National Trust open space, and follow the path downhill to small road where we turn left.

We are soon at a road junction, where we cross to the National Trust sign (Headley Heath) taking the left hand footpath going uphill. Later, when the path flattens, we pass a holly hedge on our left and turn right on a surfaced drive. Opposite a very large house on the right we turn left on a small grass path, soon turning right at a crossing path down an open area and after crossing a bridleway, we turn left at a T-junction.

After about 500 yards we go steeply uphill to a T-junction where we turn right along the top of a ridge and almost immediately we turn left to go downhill on a path later with steps. At the bottom we turn right on a main bridleway and as this begins to go uphill we go under a barrier on the left to a pleasant grassy footpath which later gradually gains height. After about half a mile we go under a barrier and turn left through another barrier up a track, ignoring side turnings.

Reaching an open area with a junction of six broad paths we take the second on the right which soon becomes a wide gravel track later going downhill and uphill. At the top of the rise we take the second path on the left which becomes grassy. We enjoy the views and after about 50 yards or so the path forks and we take the right fork into trees.

We come into the open and maintaining direction over a crossing track we eventually reach a main crossing track which we cross diagonally left into an open area. Passing a left turning we bear right towards an area of trees and then take the left fork soon bearing left and passing a water trough over to the right. When the path forks again we take the left fork and at a crossing track turn right keeping straight ahead to take the next right fork. Eventually, on reaching a junction of several paths, we take the second on the left with a seat on our right shortly reaching the car park.

Refreshments: Canteen at the Headley Heath car park. the Cock Horse and a village store in Headley village.

WALK 16

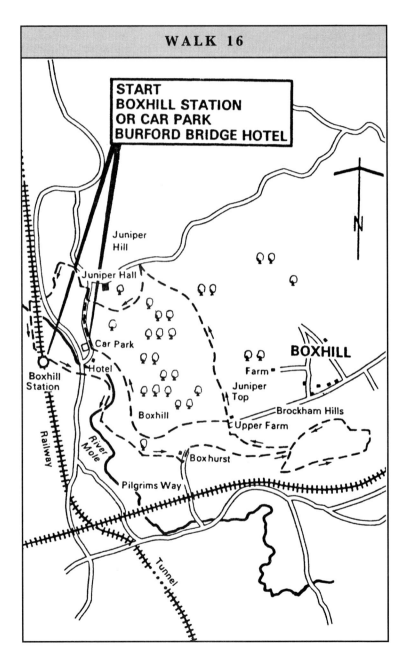

START
BOXHILL STATION
OR CAR PARK
BURFORD BRIDGE HOTEL

Juniper
Hill

Juniper Hall

Car Park

Hotel

Boxhill
Station

Railway

River Mole

Boxhill

Pilgrims Way

Boxhurst

Tunnel

BOXHILL

Farm

Juniper
Top

Brockham Hills

Upper Farm

N

BOXHILL

(i) Boxhill, Duke's Plantation, Juniper Top. 5³⁄₄ miles
(ii) Boxhill, Brockham Hills, The Whites. 6 miles

The two different endings can be interchanged, thus giving a short walk of 4¹⁄₂ miles or a more strenuous walk of 7¹⁄₂ miles.

These two walks will greatly increase our appreciation of the beauty of the Boxhill area. They are suitable for any time of the year but will give most pleasure in early summer when the chalk downland flowers and butterflies abound, or in the autumn when we can enjoy the changing colours of trees and shrubs. The longer walk goes steeply up and down hill several times. Remember that the chalk slopes can be slippery when wet.

How to get there: By bus to Burford Bridge Hotel. By train to Boxhill station. By car to the Burford Bridge car park (1 mile north of Dorking on the A24).

From the station:

Leaving Boxhill station we turn right down the road to the main road, crossing by a subway, turning left and at the subway sign taking a small path on our right.

From the car park and Burford Bridge Hotel:

We walk towards Dorking along the main road, over the river and left at the subway sign.

For both walks:

A grassy track takes us to the River Mole and we follow the riverside path with the steep wooded side of Boxhill towering above us. This is a beautiful stretch of the river, much frequented by fishermen. We cross the river by an iron bridge erected by the Ramblers' Association in memory of their members who fell in the 1939-45 war. (As an alternative, we may go a little further along and cross by the stepping stones but these are sometimes flooded. From the stepping stones we go forward a short distance until the path from the bridge joins in on the left.)

Leaving the bridge we take the forward path away from the river and at a T-junction in about 100 yards we turn left and soon go uphill bearing right. We climb steeply upward on a stepped path passing, on our right, a North Downs Way post. We bear left up a second flight of steps and at a waymark post on the left, we take a small path on the right into trees. This sloping path goes round the contour of the hill through trees, until we finally emerge over a stile into the open.

We continue in the same direction on a small path round the contour of Boxhill with trees on our right. In the summer this chalky downland area abounds in wild flowers and butterflies. (Alternatively, for good views, we turn immediately right and in a few yards left and continue through trees with good views on the right.) Our path eventually bears right (straight on if we went through the trees) down to a gate and stile over which we continue down to join a track to a drive on which we turn left uphill, soon taking a footpath on the right parallel with the drive. Later we turn right on a track which goes uphill and takes us round the side of the hill. After about 1 mile on this pleasant track, we reach a sharp hairpin bend in an area known as Duke's Plantation.

For the shorter walk:

We go round the hairpin bend and, after a quarter of a mile, at a gate, we turn left down steps and shortly right at an acorn sign. We continue round the wooded hillside and at a crossing path turn right, soon reaching the road with Upper Farm Caravan Park opposite.

For the longer walk:

The hairpin bend turns left but we take a smaller path on the right going steeply down steps to a bridleway where we turn right. Going steeply downhill we reach a crossing path by a wartime pillbox and turn left. This path leads us to a clearing which we cross, with old limekilns on our left and some buildings on our right. We take the path on the right of the limekilns and continue with a wire fence on our right. Avoiding branching paths we soon have open fields visible through the fringe of trees on our right. At a signposted staggered junction, with a stile into a field on our right, we fork left and soon go steeply uphill keeping on the main path until we reach a major chalky crossing track where we turn left gently uphill with some fine views.

Just before the top, at a signpost, we turn left up steps to visit a gravestone on our right inscribed 'Quick'. 29.9.36 to 22.10.44. An English thoroughbred'. We continue past the grave on a small footpath with a caravan site on our right and after a while our path joins a bridleway on which we bear left.

This track soon goes steeply downhill and later we turn right up some steps by an acorn sign and follow an uphill path with a handrail soon coming out on the bridleway through Duke's Plantation at the hairpin bend. We now rejoin the shorter walk and follow it to the road with Upper Farm caravan park opposite.

For both walks we have a choice of two ways back to Burford Bridge Hotel:

(A) *Over 'The Whites' 1½ miles*

We turn left on the road for a few yards to a National Trust sign where we turn left on a small path into trees, soon turning right on a path parallel with the road. We follow the acorn signs (North Downs Way) as far as the memorial viewpoint on Boxhill. From this we bear right to the road where we continue for about 150 yards. Just past the National Trust Information Centre and Tea Gardens we turn left at a signpost and when this path forks it does not matter which fork we take: one goes past old fortifications and they both come out to the well-known white chalk track over the top of Boxhill. Noticing the views of Ranmore common and Ranmore church spire ahead, we go downhill on the ridge towards a red-tiled house, and nearing the foot of the hill we bear left to the car park and Burford Bridge Hotel.

(B) *Over Juniper Top to Boxhill Station 3 miles*

Crossing the road diagonally left; we go forward with the boundary fence of the caravan park on our right, later turning right with the fence. We soon turn left with the path and continue for about three quarters of a mile, ignoring side turnings. We finally emerge into the open space of Juniper Top, with fine views of Mickleham Downs straight ahead and Ranmore common on the left. We keep to the open space in the centre of this shoulder of hill and go downhill on a gradual slope, with thick trees, mostly yews, on our left, and later birch trees. At the bottom of the hill the path enters a wooded area and we come out through a kissing gate into Juniper Bottom, where we turn left, doubling back along the valley. On our right we have a tree fringed field and then a small wooded area. Just before an open slope we take a narrow path on the right into woods. (This is **not** the path outside the wood with the open space on the left.)

The path in the woods goes steeply uphill and at the top we

ignore a left turning. Our track bears right, passes a house, Pinehurst, in trees on our left and finally winds down to the road which we cross to some steps opposite. These lead to a path parallel with the road. Later, on the right, we pass Juniper Hall, a Surrey County Council Field Studies Centre. We rejoin the road after about a quarter of a mile, continue direction for about 30 yards then turn left on an enclosed footpath bearing left down some steps and through a kissing gate. We go forward along the edge of a field with the hedge, and after another kissing gate, a wooden fence on our left. We cross a stile and a drive diagonally left to an enclosed footpath at the side of a bungalow. This takes us down to the main road (A24), which we cross with care, to a path immediately opposite.

After going under a railway bridge, we turn left then over a bridge crossing the River Mole, continuing on a grassy path with the railway embankment on our left. A kissing stile takes us to an enclosed path leading to the road where we turn left to Boxhill station a few yards away, or continue down the road to the main road and subway to Burford Bridge Hotel.

Refreshments: Restaurant and bar at Upper Farm caravan park, National Trust tearoom at the top of Boxhill, Burford Bridge Hotel, the Stepping Stones pub on the road from Boxhill station, and the cafe in Burford Bridge car park.

WALK 17

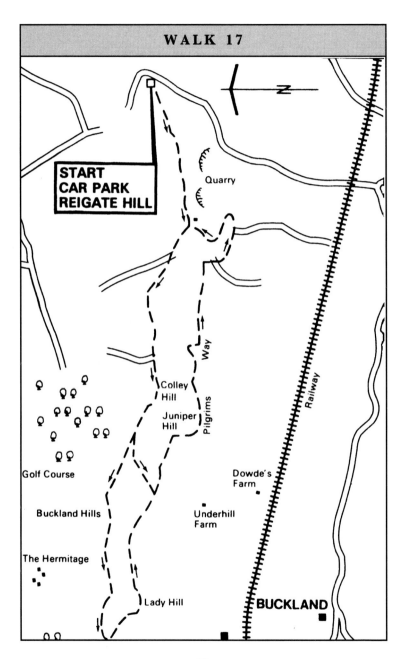

START
CAR PARK
REIGATE HILL

Quarry

Way

Railway

Colley
Hill

Juniper
Hill

Pilgrims

Golf Course

Dowde's
Farm

Buckland Hills

Underhill
Farm

The Hermitage

Lady Hill

BUCKLAND

REIGATE HILL

Reigate Hill, Colley Hill, Buckland Hills
4$\frac{1}{2}$ or 6$\frac{3}{4}$ miles

In this walk, we explore the breezy slopes of Reigate and Colley hills, with wide panoramic views, continue along the Buckland Hills and return on the ancient trackway at the foot of this range of hills. While being enjoyable at any season, the walk is particularly beautiful in autumn when the beeches at the foot of Colley Hill are changing colour. The path down through the Buckland Hills, for the shorter walk, is steep and might be best avoided in wet conditions.

How to get there: By bus to the top of Reigate Hill. By car to the car park at the top of Reigate Hill on the A217.

From the car park, we make for the footbridge over the main road, passing the refreshment hut and toilets on our right. We follow this tree-lined track for about three quarters of a mile, passing a water tower on our right, and coming out at the open top and non-functional memorial fountain of Colley Hill.

Noticing the slopes of Leith Hill in the distance, we continue along this grassy hilltop, keeping near the edge of the escarpment. As we are approaching the end of the open area we bear right into scrub on a well defined path. We are soon at a National Trust sign 'Colley Hill', where we turn left on a wide track with fencing on the left. After keeping left and left again at forks we shortly come out to a small tarmac drive where we turn left and almost at once, opposite brick gateposts, turn right on an enclosed path. We continue on this along the top of Juniper Hill for about a third of a mile, with occasional glimpses of views.

For the shorter walk:

We take the footpath on the left going down through the Buckland Hills, at first with a holly hedge on the right and wire fence on the left. At the end of the fence we go through yews and soon very steeply downhill, coming suddenly out into the open with wonderful views. We continue downhill towards a clump of trees and just before the bottom go down some steps and turn left on a crossing track which is part of the ancient trackway running along the foot of this range of hills.

For the longer walk:

At the footpath sign on the left we maintain our original direction and are soon walking along the top of the Buckland Hills with the back of an occasional house on the left and open fields visible through a fringe of trees on our right. Later the path enters a wooded area and soon emerges into the open, giving fine views of the Betchworth Clump, with the Redland Heights and slopes of Leith Hill in the distance. On a clear day, the South Downs are visible on the horizon.

Continuing with a fenced wood on our right, the path soon turns left for a short way downhill and then right again, thus skirting a rectangular field by turning right up the third side. Our path leaves the rectangular field and bears left into woods, soon going uphill for a short distance then resuming direction. Eventually our track meets a major bridleway on which we turn left downhill, with steep banks on either side. Our path, bordered by ancient yews, bears left and, at a North Downs Way sign, we turn left up a stepped path. This leads round the base of the hills we walked over earlier and now we are walking on an open path through an area noted in summer for its variety of wild flowers and butterflies.

We continue forward at the foot of the hills, sometimes in the open sand sometimes under trees. We ignore a path forking right to Underhill Farm and very soon we are joined on the left by a path ending in steps coming down from the Buckland Hills.

Both walks now follow the same route:

Later, having walked round the foot of Juniper Hill, we continue over a crossing track and go through barriers to a yew-lined track following the path which twists and turns round the foot of Colley Hill.

At Colley Pits we ignore a fork on our left and go down some steps, still keeping along the foot of the hill, ignoring all turnings off. We finally come out to a tarmac road, and go under a wooden barrier, still maintaining our direction. In about 100 yards, as the road turns right, we fork left towards a house, Underbeeches, and turn sharply left again with a beech hedge on the left and a wall on the right. We continue uphill to a granite memorial obelisk and when the track levels out we turn right up some steps which bring us back to the memorial fountain on Colley Hill which we passed earlier. Turning right we retrace our steps along the bridleway back to the car park.

Refreshments: The refreshment hut in the car park at the top of Reigate Hill

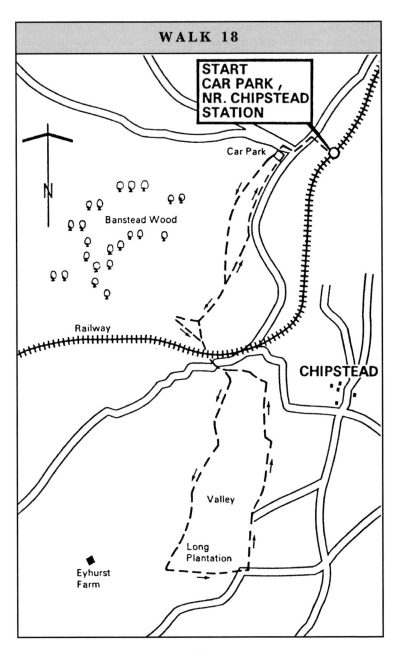

WALK 18

START
CAR PARK ,
NR. CHIPSTEAD
STATION

Car Park

N

Banstead Wood

Railway

CHIPSTEAD

Valley

Long
Plantation

Eyhurst
Farm

CHIPSTEAD VALLEY

Chipstead Valley and Long Plantation
4½ miles

This walk is in a delightful area, very close to London, with wild flowers on the hillside and good views across the valley.

How to get there: By train to Chipstead railway station, going down Station Approach, turning left on the main road and right down Lower Park Road to the car park on the left. By bus to Chipstead Valley alighting at the Midday Sun pub, walking half a mile along the road signposted to Banstead and turning right down Lower Park Road.

By car to the Banstead Woods car park at the end of Holly Lane (B2219).

We leave the car park by the kissing gate with toilets on our left and take an uphill path on the *outside* of Banstead Woods. We remain on this path for about 1 mile, without entering the woods, enjoying good views.

Later, we reach open hillside with a field on our right and a fringe of trees and downward slope on our left. As the field on the right ends, our path turns left and we go forward a few yards to a junction of paths. We take the path on the extreme right with fine views across the valley on our left. On reaching a post we double back on the left on a lower footpath along open hillside: this is a small diversion to enjoy really fine views. Later we go over a crossing track and soon join the path which was on the extreme left of the recent junction of paths. We turn right downhill then cross the railway. At the road we bear slightly left to cross to a kissing gate opposite.

We go forward with a garden fence on our right but as the fence turns a corner we maintain direction and bear right up a slope to a gate which takes us through a narrow strip of woods and out to a field. After bearing right uphill round the edge of this field we turn right into Long Plantation, a Surrey County Council Open Space. In a few yards we turn left on a wide track for about a mile.

After going slightly uphill, we go down and at a well-defined waymarked crossing path we turn left going downhill crossing the valley. At a gate we take the signposted permissive footpath uphill besides the hedge and at the top turn left on a path which leads us back along the other side of the valley.

When our path is joined by a track coming in on the right, we continue forward with woods on our right and the open valley on our left. We have practically completed our return on the other side of the valley when we continue through a small gate. We maintain direction across an open field until we are opposite a stile up on our right. Here, we turn left downhill to the gate and the road which we crossed earlier.

We now retrace our steps, crossing the railway and continuing straight up the uphill path, ignoring a path on the left, to the top where we turn right with a field on our left and hedgerow on our right. Shortly we turn right on a crossing track going downhill with trees on our left.

At the end of the hedge we turn left and go forward across the downs with trees over to our left and parallel with the road a short distance away on our right, and we finally go through a kissing gate to the car park. (Toilet facilities are available at the car park.)

Refreshments: The Midday Sun in Chipstead Valley Road, or the Ramblers Rest, Outwood Lane.

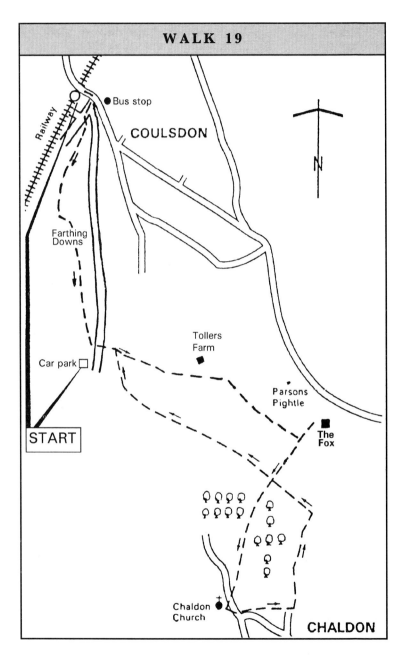

COULSDON

Farthing Downs, Happy Valley and Chaldon
5½ miles

The Green Belt area of Farthing Downs and Happy Valley belongs to the Corporation of London and is managed by the Kent and Surrey Commons. This lovely area of chalk downland has been designated as a Site of Special Scientific Interest (SSSI) on account of the great variety of flora and fauna found here.

How to get there: By train to Coulsdon South railway station. By bus to Downs Road off Marlpit Lane. By car to the car park a mile up the Farthing Downs road on the right.

From the car park at the top of Farthing Downs we would recommend walking back to the millennium cairn and picking up the walk from there.

From Coulsdon South station:

The downside platform gives access to Reddown Road where we turn left to Marlpit Lane, turn right and soon right up Downs Road. There are many tracks going south over Farthing Downs and a small tarmac road for cars. We go through gate number 26 and keep to the side slopes well over to the right where the Downs Road houses are partly screened by a fringe of yew trees. As Westwood Road joins Downs Road, we turn diagonally left up a grassy track, which leads uphill to the highest part of Farthing Downs where there are some trees and a signpost. Here, we turn right for a short distance to the millenium cairn viewpoint.

We maintain direction along this wide grassy track and later the area known as Happy Valley can be seen ahead on the left. Just before fencing we turn left, cross the road and take the third gate on our right to go diagonally downhill. We cross a bridleway through white posts, continue downhill and cross another bridleway. This narrow path descends an open hillside with many downland flowers.

We turn right along the valley bottom and shortly at a fork keep left on the wide horse track, soon taking a small uphill path on the left. Just before the top turn right on a narrow crossing path with woods on the left and fine views down the valley on our right. Later our path enters woods but we turn right then bear left downhill with trees on our left. We continue over a crossing track at the bottom then go uphill past some seats on the right, maintaining direction on the right-hand of two paths. Keeping along the top of the open downs, at a signpost we turn right down a path, which soon becomes stepped, and cross the valley with a hedge on our left.

After going through a strip of woodland, we continue on a well-defined path over fields. Eventually we reach the road where we turn left and right almost at once on a small approach road leading to the church of St Peter and St Paul, Chaldon.

This ancient church, which dates back to 1100, contains many treasures, such as a 600 year old tomb, and a tablet inscribed in 1562, but chief among these is the unique and remarkable mural painted in 1170 but only discovered in 1870, under a preserving coat of whitewash.

Leaving the church by the other approach road on the right go down to a road which we cross to a signposted footpath on a track with open fields on the left and the backs of houses on the right. Soon we have a wood on our left and, on reaching a crossing lane, we turn left with the wood on our left and houses and gardens on the right. At the last house the lane becomes a footpath and enters the wood, sloping slightly downhill for about a quarter of a mile until the valley becomes visible on our left.

Here we leave our track which continues downhill while we go over a stile, turning left along the open hillside with woods on our left. We are soon back at the hedge which spans the valley and we pass through a gap keeping up on the hillside with woods on our left and the valley bottom on our right. Our path takes us through a small wooded strip and out into the open again and we maintain direction. We re-enter the woods and our wide track leads us out to a house with the car park and toilets to our left and interesting information panels nearby.

We retrace our steps along Farthing Downs back to the bus stop and station.

Refreshments: The Fox (turning left at the signposted stepped path).

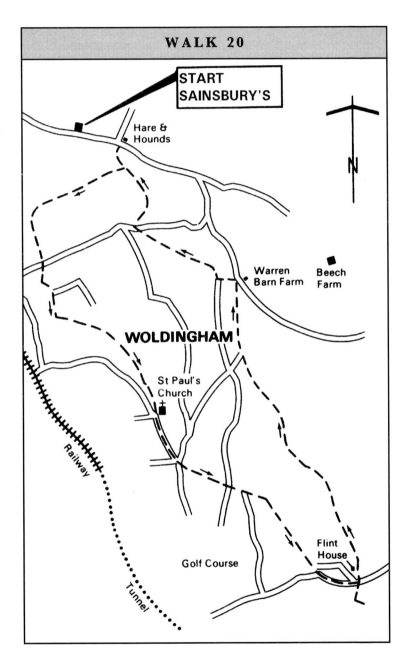

WALK 20

START SAINSBURY'S

Hare & Hounds

N

Warren Barn Farm

Beech Farm

WOLDINGHAM

St Paul's Church

Railway

Tunnel

Golf Course

Flint House

92

CHELSHAM

Chelsham toWoldingham and back
6³/₄ miles

This is a fairly hilly but pleasant walk for any time of the year. In summer, there are plenty of chalkland flowers and butterflies on the downs and field footpaths.

How to get there: By bus to the Hare and Hounds at Chelsham. There is ample parking space nearby.

Opposite the Hare and Hounds, we cross the grass diagonally left and follow a tarmac lane, turning right along Plantation Lane and continuing on the main track with the valley on the left. After just over half a mile we take the first stile on the left near the clubhouse in the valley and go across the golf course up to a stile to the right of trees, cross the road and go uphill beside a fence to a stile under trees. We come out to a small residential road where we continue direction and as the road turns left we go forward on a footpath crossing another small road. We continue forward, go down steps then keep left through a wooden barrier for about half a mile, with occasional seats, woods on our left and a valley on our right with good views. The last part of the path is fenced and eventually comes out to a wider lane where we maintain direction to St Paul's church, Woldingham.

Built in 1933, this church is well worth a visit. The bluish agates set in the inscription above the altar were a gift from

Hyderabad, and the stained glass windows above the altar depict the sea in various moods. The roof timbers of Colombian pine support concealed lighting and the windows are surrounded with dressed flints.

With the church on our left, we continue along the road, past shops, to Woldingham Green and fork left down Upper Court Road. Just past a house called Sylvan Mount, we turn left down a steep path, passing a house on the right at the bottom of a dip. We cross the lane to Southview Road and, just past a house, turn slightly left to a signposted footpath.

We follow this path for about half a mile finally going uphill with trees on our left and over a stile to a road. We cross over and turn left to glimpse the view over Oxted from the old road, following it to a junction where we take the road signposted Oxted and Limpsfield. Continuing on this for a short distance, we then take a footpath on the left downhill to the top of Oxted Downs for views and a rest.

Retracing our steps back to the road, we turn right and back to the crossroads and continue on Flint House Lane, the bridleway to Warlingham, passing Flint House on our left. We maintain direction on this bridleway for a good mile: the last half mile has woods on the right and is often rather muddy. Eventually we emerge at the top of a wide sloping field and go downhill on a clear path and out to the road.

We turn right passing some houses and later, opposite Warren Barn Farm, we turn left along Upland Road. At the T-junction we turn right along a pleasant residential road out to Slines New Road. Here, we cross to a bridleway opposite, which takes us uphill and finally back to the green space opposite the Hare and Hounds at Chelsham.

Refreshments: Confectionery and ice cream at Woldingham village and Chelsham.